"Many people get stuck in a routine and path for their lives that does not give them the levels of contribution, happiness, and fulfillment that they hoped their lives would have. Their hopes and beliefs about what is possible for their lives narrows and so dreams and goals are not pursued.

Robin Marvel's book, *Life Check*, will help you shed the excuses you have been using and give you the tools you need to master your thoughts, emotions, and actions so that you discover your Purpose and Passion and pursue it with zeal."

Tom Cunningham
Napoleon Hill Certified Instructor
Canada's Leading *Think and Grow Rich* Expert

I0026746

Praise for Robin Marvel's *Life Check*

"*Life Check* is the perfect resource for motivation, inspiration, and a reassurance that the life we are looking for is clearly within our reach. Through her use of relatable examples, Robin clearly lays out a no-nonsense, but spectacularly stirring plan for the success that is waiting for all. If you're looking for a practical and realistic guide to help you get started on the journey to self discovery and self mastery on the way to the success that awaits, this book is exactly what you're looking for!"

Victor Schueller,
Professor of Positivity and Possibility
www.VictorSchueller.com

"Robin Marvel is a walking, talking example of how one can overcome a life of struggle no matter what your circumstances are or have been. She has gleaned her wisdom from life's experiences and has so graciously shared it all in her book *Life Check*.

If you are seriously ready to make the changes necessary to create the authentic life you deserve and don't quite know where to begin, I urge you to read and implement the loving guidance contained in this easy to read, straightforward book.

If life isn't ticking all your boxes, this 'how to' book will assist you to change that. *Life Check...* check it out!"

Rinnell Kelly, *Scents of Wellbeing*

"*Life Check* gives you the questions to reflect on and really think about to be able to achieve your dreams. Reading this has opened my mind to yet another stage of understanding myself better. *Life Check* gives you clear step-by-step instructions to be able to look at your life and find your balance. This book came to me at the perfect time—when I was in a very unbalanced place in my life. I have read this book twice now and get something new out of it each time.

Robin Marvel is truly an amazing and inspiring woman who shares her journey in hopes to touch just one person and change their life! She has done that for me twice now, her books have helped me overcome some obstacles in my life when I thought that I wasn't going to make it out."

Sheila LaBrie,
Empowerment Workshop attendee

"If there is a label in society given to Robin Marvel it is of an Angel here to assist others in their life journey of awareness and empowerment.

With each exercise in *Life Check*, you find the mask that you wear is not of your own choosing, but rather the choice that you have embraced. Once again Robin shares her innermost strengths to show you how to step up and take action in your life by utilizing seven self-loving steps to rise above."

Adele Marie, *Angelic Wise Ones*
www.AngelicWiseOnes.com

LIFE
Check

7 STEPS TO
BALANCE YOUR LIFE!

ROBIN MARVEL

ISBN 978-1-61599-204-1: paperback
ISBN 978-1-61599-205-8: eBook

From the Modern Spirituality Series
www.MarvelousSpirit.com
Marvelous Spirit Press, an imprint of

Loving Healing Press
5145 Pontiac Trail
Ann Arbor, MI 48105
Tollfree 888-761-6268 (USA/CAN)
FAX 734-663-6861

Library of Congress Cataloging-in-Publication
Data

Marvel, Robin, 1979-
 Life check : 7 steps to balance your life! / Robin
Marvel.
     pages cm -- (The modern spirituality series)
  Includes bibliographical references and index.
  ISBN 978-1-61599-204-1 (trade paper : alk.
paper) -- ISBN 978-1-61599-205-8 (ebook)
 1. Self-actualization (Psychology) I. Title.
  BF637.S4M3675 2013
  158.1--dc23
                                    2013021592

Dedicated to all the people who keep me motivated by believing in who I am.

Especially Keith and our five amazing daughters who always give me a reason to keep believing in myself.

Contents

Life Checks

Introduction

The world is full of people waiting to be successful. They are waiting for the time to be right to take the move forward in their lives. They wait for life to come to them instead of creating a life they want. The excuse can be for the weather to be right, to lose the ten pounds, for the economy, for the timing to be perfect before they are ready to take life head on. Does this sound familiar to you? Are you allowing excuses to create limits and be the reason you are not going after what you desire in your life? If you are like most people, you can honestly answer this with a yes.

I too was that person, finding excuses to justify why I was not moving forward toward my goals. Then one day I looked at my life of struggle and unhappiness and made the choice to take personal responsibility for achieving my dreams. I realized I could gain success and live the life I imagined if I was open to make the changes I needed, do the work that comes with change and be committed to my personal success.

Being successful is not about being rich, it is not about being in power, it is about a combination of all you have to offer and the commitment you are willing to make to accomplish all you desire.

In life, you must focus on all areas of who you are, keeping mind, body and spirit balanced. Creating strength in all aspects of your character from personal responsibility to goal setting to achieving. Leaving out any area removes your opportunity for success.

This book will show you how to embrace all areas of who you are, amplifying your strengths and transforming your weaknesses.

Life Check is written for the everyday people that the world belongs to, the people like you and I who are working every day to live passionately and to experience a life full of happiness, success and joy. It provides many tried and true methods that I learned the hard way—you know, the old school way of trial-and-error. Now I want to share them with you so you can skip the trial-and-error, wasting no time and start to experience joy, passion, empowerment and happiness in your daily living.

I have personally watched my experience and that of others drastically change when making the commitment to learn and apply the methods outlined in this book. They create a strategic way to accomplish anything you want, empowering you to take a Life Check and to put you in the dominant role in your life.

Throughout the chapters of this book, there will be opportunities for you to stop and take a Life Check—a series of questions and thinking points that will help you to slow down and check where you are at present. I recommend you create a journal that will help you to keep track of your progress and for reference as you move forward toward success.

We have all had struggles that have left us complaining and whining, and it is easy to let these obstacles control the remainder of our days—always feeling as if we are getting the shaft from life, that the world is out to get us. Today, as you begin this book, you will start to discover that how you are approaching and dealing with the challenges of your life will determine the successes you experience.

If you are willing to commit yourself to learning the tools presented in this book, you will discover that YOU have the power to change your life, YOU have the power to live in a passionate, motivated, positive way that YOU control. By adding the steps from *Life Check* into your daily living you will see an amazing improvement in all areas.

This is your how-to book on ways to create and live a successful, motivated and passionate life. There will be no more waiting for the door to open when you have the key safely tucked away in your pocket. So, today approach that door and unlock your greatest potential.

1 – Rock the Boat

"Men are afraid to rock the boat in which they hope to drift safely through life's currents, when, actually, the boat is stuck on a sandbar. They would be better off to rock the boat and try to shake it loose."

~Thomas Szasz

Your life is not happening to you, it is respond-
ing to you. Your actions, the choices you make,
your thoughts and the words you speak determine
the quality of your of life. So then, who are you
and how is your life treating you?

Figuring out who you are in truth will reveal so
much about you and the path you are on. Every
moment, every choice you make is directly related
to how you see yourself, who you believe you are
and what you think you are worth. These three
factors determine everything—what you work to
accomplish, whom you marry, your daily routine,
how you limit and label yourself, how you treat
others and all that you allow to take place in your
life.

Life Check 1-1: Valuing the Self

- ✓ What do you think you are worth?
- ✓ How do you value yourself?
- ✓ Are you worth an amazing life, deserving to get all the things that you desire?
- ✓ Are you worth your dreams?
- ✓ Do you deserve the respect of yourself and others?

These are challenging questions that encourage you to really look at yourself, and you may not be able to answer them right now. However, by the end of this book you will see yourself, your relationships and your life with more value and you'll answer these questions with confidence and positivity.

In order to figure out who you are and how you value yourself, you must take a look at the real you. This is the person standing when you take away the job, the marital status, the family, the labels, the programmed beliefs: the true, down to the core individual. This is who speaks to you in silence and looks back at you from the mirror, giving you the chance to see yourself clearly.

If you are unable to see your worth, you will slowly lose your confidence and you'll begin to just exist. It is like a balloon that is full of air that gets a pinhole in it—it will slowly deflate until there is nothing left. The same thing happens in life if you don't value yourself. If this sounds like your situation, then I am sure glad you picked up this book so we can patch that pin hole and refill your balloon with a zest for life!

As you struggle with your self-worth, you may become stagnant, losing that inner spark and passion. Then life becomes routine, just going through the motions—get up, go to work, complain about the weather, complain about your job, what your spouse didn't do, your house, your kids, eat lunch, complain about co-workers, drive home, make dinner, put kids to bed, veg out on TV programs you idolize because the people are living with the excitement you crave but are scared to go after, go to bed and start over tomorrow.

When you are asked how your day is you are quick to respond with "so- so—you know, paying the bills." This is so common because it is always easier to stay in the comfort zone of your routine rather than walking outside that bubble and testing the waters. You always have that little bit of nagging doubt, the "what if" thoughts running around in the back of your mind. These thoughts may question if you are worth the great things in life, because you are totally focused on working so hard to make ends meet. You want to be comfortable, which can be a great thing but it becomes restricting when you lose sight of your passions and give up on yourself. Your life iPod gets stuck on playing the same two or three songs on repeat.

You no longer wake up in the morning saying, "Yes! Another amazing day to be alive!" Instead you become use to what is, settling because it is familiar and works, so why rock the boat. Well, I want you to stand up and rock your boat, dive back into life and regain your passion and purpose!

Life Check 1-2: Self-Critic

Pause for a moment and go look in the mirror. As you look at yourself,

- ✓ What thoughts pop into your head? Are they negative?

- ✓ Do you find yourself being a self critic? Be honest with yourself.

- ✓ Make the choice to stop the negative self chatter. Replace any negative words you are thinking about yourself with positive affirmations. The more you practice replacing negative thoughts with positive affirmations, the sooner they will leave. You are reprogramming the beliefs you hold for yourself.

So, now that you are taking a real, deep look at your genuine self, you will discover your self-worth, not the worth others have of you but what you really feel your value is.

Pay attention to the part of you that's visible when you shed the need to fit in, the fake image you project to others and the need for approval: the authentic you. Your life is created from the inside out, so when facing yourself you are able to really uncover the truth because you cannot lie. You can always step into the world with a smile and when asked "how are you" reply with a "great" but when you have to be honest there is no way to fool yourself. The truth is revealed and you cannot ignore it no matter how many masks you may wear in the outside world. You can walk around like you are on top of the world but if in the shadows of your truth you are lacking confidence, full of fear and worry, then you cannot truly experience a life of positivity, confidence and fearlessness—your genuine truth shines through in all aspects of your life. It is the real you. This is the you that was whole at one time, the you that unconditionally loved yourself and seen how beautiful you really are; the you that got excited and felt passionate.

Life Check 1-3: Passion

✓   Do you remember that person?

✓   When was the last time your spirit was on fire?

You are shaped by the positive and negative, internal and external events that you face throughout your daily living. The emotions and reactions you experience through each of these life circumstances creates your behavior and ultimately becomes how you deal with your life. It is imperative to take a look at those defining moments, positive and negative, to find the answers to why your life is how it is. As you experience negative moments you develop self doubt, fear and do not live your truth. This takes a toll on your self-worth. As you are experiencing positive moments you are strengthening your true self, empowering who you are to live an amazing life.

Unfortunately, life is not only full of positive moments but negative ones as well. Learning how to heal from old negative experiences and how to react to new negative experiences is the key to being in control of your life.

Life Check 1-4: Wounded Eye

✓ Think of negative events you have faced.

✓ How did you react? Was your reaction healthy?

Believe it or not, there was a powerful, confident you before doubts crept in, before you developed a *wounded eye* from traumatic circumstances you have faced. There are many outside factors that have had an emotional impact on who you are today.

Let's take a look at some outside factors that may have affected you:

- Being bullied
- Abandonment
- Rejection of any kind
- Dealing with physical, mental, emotional abuse from others
- Self destruction with negative thoughts and words
- Loss
- Substance abuse of any kind

All these experiences slowly start to deplete your passion for life, creating self doubt and your get up and go energy, causing a wounded eye to form.

As you are encountering trauma, tragedy and hardship, you start to create your wounded eye, and if you aren't careful you can continue to live your life looking through it, carrying the emotion from each of these experiences into your daily living, defining yourself and your life from the negative emotion or wounded eye. Every time anything happens to you in the present, you relive the feelings of heartache that you experienced, using these old emotions as excuses for where you are in life now. It allows you to stay limited and stuck because you tell yourself that you have a good reason for being self destructive. Then society empowers you by giving you permission to stay wounded.

Life Check 1-5: Letting Go Excuses

✓ What experiences do you hold on to as an excuse for where your life is today?

✓ Are you ready to see clearly by healing your wounded eye?

How many times have you heard a story of someone who is exhibiting negative behavior like alcoholism, and then you hear yourself or others say, "That's so sad, but you know his mother died when he was fifteen so it makes sense." We as a society give permission to those who suffer trauma, creating an excuse and contributing to their wounded eye. I too have done that in the past until I realized I was encouraging self destructive behavior. It is important for you to stop making excuses for yourself and also for others. There is no reason to lose today by looking through the wounded eye of yesterday.

Have you ever seen the A&E network show *Intervention*? It is a great example of how common it is for people to live looking through their wounded eye. The majority of people on that show facing an intervention, no matter how old or what they are addicted to, always place blame for where they are now on something that happened 5, 10, or 15 plus years ago. Their lists include "my father never hugged me," "my parents divorced," "my dad was an alcoholic," "I was abused," "my mom abandoned us," "my sister stole my boyfriend" ...All of these are classic examples of someone living through their wounded eye. Their present life is in shambles, filled with addiction to fill the void created in the past when they experienced trauma, or had their feelings hurt or someone let them down. They are so quick to use this as an excuse to live through their wounded eye. Every experience they encounter in the present they react with the same behavior they had during the past trauma, creating a repetitive pattern. They see everything through the emotion of the past circumstance. This allows an excuse, as well as someone to blame for their present conditions.

I grew up with alcoholic, cocaine abusing parents. Their drug abuse ruled our life and left us homeless several times. I could easily choose to repeat the cycle and be an alcoholic or a drug abuser and blame it on my childhood. Society would defend me, claiming it makes sense because I had such an unstable childhood. I have made the choice to heal my wounded eye and not accept that as my truth, and I chose to break the cycle. Your rough past does not have to reflect on who you choose to be now. I am proof of that!

I am not saying that you have not faced hardships that can slow you down and change your course, what I am saying is that you have the choice to give your power away in the present to these past emotions or to release them and gain power. You can live looking through your wounded eye, or heal it. The choice is yours. You are solely responsible for how your life plays out.

Once you make the decision to clear your wounded eye, be prepared, it takes lots of work. It is not just a flip of the switch but an intense commitment to start taking personal responsibility for yourself. You need dedication to stop bringing your old wounds into your present. Look at it this way, if your past was so bad then why are you giving it so much space in your today? You are allowing these old emotions to rule your present and I know why. The reason you are losing so much of your present to the old stuff is because you need the excuse. If you are unhappy now, it is easier to blame it on something or someone else then to face it. That way it is not your fault. Well, it's time to wake up because no matter how many excuses you make, your life is yours and you are responsible for it.

You may not have been told this growing up, I know I wasn't. Growing up I learned that life happens to you, you are a victim of circumstance and you have no choice. Throughout my child-hood and young adult days I always saw life as a struggle and felt there was nothing I could do to change that. This continued until I was twenty-three. I remember sitting in my living room and reading a book titled *Choosing Happiness: The Art of Living Unconditionally* (1991) by Veronica Ray and having a life changing experience. I learned that I was in control of my life. If I wanted to be happy then it was up to me, that for years I had been putting the burden of my happiness on my husband, the weather, my job, anything or anyone I could. Wow, that blew my mind! So I decided to put my newfound information into practice and it was game on! I made the choice to take personal responsibility for my life.

At first it was not easy because of course it was easier for me to blame others for where I was at. The more I committed myself to making personal changes, the more my life started to change for the positive. This choice changed every aspect of who I am today. I became more confident and started to create the life I desired, because if it was up to me, there was no way I was going to continue to sit on the sidelines and not participate in living. So here I am, telling you that in order to gain success in any area, you must take personal responsibility for where you have been and where you are going.

Life Check 1-6: Responsibility

✓ Are you taking responsibility for your life?

✓ If not, who are you giving that power to?

✓ What steps can you take today to start taking personal responsibility for your life?

You are the person who should be raising a hand when the questions arise: Why is my life the way it is? Whose fault is it that I am not happy?

You are in control of your life, you hold the key to where you are and where you are heading.

Taking personal responsibility includes looking at all the choices you are making. This goes from the daily choices like brushing your hair, going to work, what's for dinner, right lane/left lane, to life-shaping, important matters.

Your basic choices keep you living from day to day and are important to your self-worth. Making the choice to get up each morning and embrace the day impacts your entire life. Taking the time to care for yourself by brushing your hair and dressing for success empowers and motivates you. No matter what you do during your day, it is important to present yourself in a way that makes you feel good. Value yourself, you are worth it.

Life Check 1-7: Choices

✓ What basic choices are you making each day that empower you?

✓ Do you start each day with a positive attitude?

✓ How can you design your daily routine to include actions that will inspire you to look and feel good?

Let's look at the main event choices in your life. You know, the ones that have defined your life up to this point and those that you are making in the present that will shape your future. These choices include all areas of your life from your career to the people you surround yourself with, to where you choose to live. It is important when you are making these main event choices that they are your truth. That is, live the life you really want, rather than living a lie to please other people. The fact is that this is your life and it is not selfish to choose your happiness and be your number one priority.

If you spend your time basing your decisions on what others want for you, you are guaranteed to complain ten years from now about what you never did while blaming someone else, creating an excuse for yourself. You'll be talking about what you could have been if only you'd followed your passions instead of following the crowd.

You have the choice right now, no matter your age, your financial situation or your past, to become anything you desire. I have watched so many people limit themselves because they believe they are too old, too young, too small town, too big town and the list goes on and on. So, no more excuses, no more self imposed limits—today you make the choices that make you feel alive. Keep in mind that your choice may change. There is nothing carved in stone saying these main life choices cannot change with your personal growth and expansion. It is foolish to chain yourself to one way in a world that is so full of opportunity. Explore. Change your mind and be okay with it. If you are spending all your time stuck in a life choice that no longer serves you, then change it. You deserve to be happy and it is up to you how you get there.

Life Check 1-8: Dreams

✓ You get excited when thinking about this dream.

✓ You are where you are right now in life because you choose...

✓ What will you commit to right now to make your dreams come true? What steps can you take right now to move forward?

2 – Leave Your Baggage

"Everyone makes mistakes, but that doesn't mean they have to pay for them the rest of their life. Sometimes good people make bad choices, it doesn't mean they're bad... It means they're human."

~Unknown

If you are like me, you have made some choices, big and small, that you'd rather not look at again, but it is important to face all aspects of who you are so you can forgive and heal. Healing is an inside job and it must start with you.

One of the most important things you can do on your path to success is to forgive yourself and others. Forgiveness is by far one of the most powerful words in existence, and will change your life forever. Although it is not always the easiest task, it is imperative to move forward and experience emotional closure.

The first thing to understand about forgiving is that it is not something you do for other people, it is something you do for yourself. It is allowing yourself to break free from the heaviness of anger and frustration. These negative emotions will eat at you physically, mentally and emotionally, taking away from your happiness.

Start with forgiving yourself. After all, you cannot give what you don't have, so if you are unable to forgive yourself, you will struggle with forgiving others.

Everyone has a past. Some are neat and tidy while others are scarred with battle wounds. If your past is one with battle wounds you have proof that no matter what you faced, it has passed and you survived! Now you need to figure out if you are willing to embrace those scars and heal them, or cover them up with a fake smile and conformity. Only you can make this choice.

Life Check 2-1: Past is Present

✓ How much of your present life are you losing to your past, to the person you use to be?

✓ Are you still blaming yourself for something you should have, could have done?

Here is a challenge for you. Carry around a suitcase full of rocks. Each boulder symbolizes an emotion like shame, guilt, should have, could have—(insert your word here) and bring this heavy burden with you everywhere you go. There is no setting it down; you must carry it at all times. Don't you think that would get exhausting? I know it would. So, why then do you insist on carrying the weight of your past like that? This is what you do when you hold on to guilt, remorse and anger for who you use to be, choices you use to make. Allowing yourself to be exhausted and defeated, struggling with the present all based on your actions in the past.

Life Check 2-2: Baggage Check

✓ Evaluate how your past baggage is preventing you from moving forward.

✓ What do you need to release, make a list and start unpacking.

You aren't the only one. We all have this baggage that we think is necessary to keep with us, holding on to it, thinking that we are better people if we feel guilty about our past actions. When you tell yourself that you must be accountable for who you were then, it allows past emotions to manipulate the present. You are your biggest critic and can really give yourself a hard time. The fact of the matter is that we have all done crazy things and said things in the past that we wish we could take back, and that is part of living and growing.

You do not get a "do-over" for the past, but you can make a choice in the present to let go of it. Forgiving yourself allows freedom from the emotional baggage, releasing the guilt and disappointment you have attached to those situations. Embrace your experiences, good and bad, and appreciate the growth they provided. Use your "get out of jail free" card and allow yourself peace of mind. Face it, you are not given a manual for living, and it can be easy to lose direction. These lessons were necessary to build your character, and to help build who you are in this moment. The fact is, you have tied so much emotion to the action you took or didn't take that you are unable to let it go. Today, look at the situation and search for the lesson that was provided. Accept the lesson, accept your choice and move forward. Finding the strength to forgive yourself will remove the heaviness you carry with you. This allows you to live life with the happiness and peace that you deserve.

Many years ago, when I was around twenty-two years old, I made the choice to go on a drinking binge, and I lost complete control of who I was. For four months I was not a very good mother or wife, because my focus was on drinking every night. I was repeating a pattern from my childhood. There were days when I didn't even see my daughter, because I was sleeping all day to prepare for the night out. When I thought of these days, I used to feel disappointed in myself, it was very unfair to the people that I love the most in my life. It would be very easy for me to carry around the energy of my past and punish myself in the present, but I made the choice to forgive myself and to learn from the experience, allowing myself to live fully in the present. I have apologized to my husband, my daughter and to myself. I realize that I am human and I learned many lessons from that point in my life and I appreciate that.

Be kind to yourself for your past choices, because they don't define who you choose to be today.

Life Check 2-3: Learning from Mistakes

- ✓ Give yourself a break. You are human and making mistakes is part of learning. So, relax and quit holding yourself hostage in your own mind.

- ✓ Look at past situations and search for the lesson that was provided to you. Accept the lesson, Accept your choice and Move Forward.

- ✓ Use what you have learned from your past to share with others facing the same situations. Encourage them by being an example that everything will be okay.

Who are you mad at? What is the one name that makes all the blood rush to your head? You probably know someone who infuriates you. This is someone, somewhere who has been rude to you and hurt you emotionally, mentally and/or physically, and you cannot imagine forgiving them. They have just caused way too much pain for you and must pay for it. You vow revenge and have lost a part of who you are to the hatred you feel.

I recently did a workshop at a domestic violence shelter and started to share the topic of forgiveness, the way I am discussing it here. I was focusing on the importance of forgiving those who have wronged you no matter the extent, not for the other person but for yourself. Encouraging the idea that forgiving others allows you to take your power back and frees you from all the hurt associated with the situation. A woman who had been battered raised her hand and said " I'll never forgive my husband for what he did to me, Never."

I responded to her by sharing that the more anger you have, the longer you hold the hatred for him, the longer he holds your power. I told her that every time she gets mad, curses him and talks about how much she cannot forgive him, he wins—because in those moments he is in control of her emotions and she is giving away her power to him by feeling that same anger she felt in that moment he abused her. She got a look on her face and told me "I haven't ever thought of that, it makes sense to me." It was her "aha" moment. Now she can move forward in her life and be free from the emotions of her abusive husband. He lost some of his hold that day! Now it'll take work, because she will have to look within and really forgive the situation but she is one step closer to freeing herself from his emotional hold.

Continuing to carry a grudge and be angry at the person who wronged you is only hurting yourself. As the great Buddha said, "Holding on to anger is like grasping a hot coal with the intent of throwing it at someone else; you are the one who gets burned." I could not agree more. Each time you harbor that anger and resentment, you lose part of your happiness. Why would you willingly sacrifice one moment, giving your power away to someone who angers you? If they were so horrible to you, do not continue to feed their negativity. Be in charge of your emotions and give no one your power. I am in no way suggesting you forget what was done to you, all I am saying is that it is time to forgive and let it go, freeing yourself. When you make that decision, you will physically feel a weight lifted from your shoulders and the relief of taking your power back.

Life Check 2-4: Forgiveness

✓ Make a list of those people you harbor anger for. List their names, what they did to you and a statement of forgiveness. I have included an example. Use as much detail as you desire when writing your statement of forgiveness. The more exact, the stronger the release.

✓ Say out loud: "I forgive _____ and appreciate the lessons I have learned from him/her." This will affirm your desire to forgive and release pent up negative energy.

3 – Raise The Bar

"Everyone is a genius, but if you judge a fish on its ability to climb a tree, it will live its whole life believing it is stupid."

~Albert Einstein

The outside voices of society place labels on everyone, along with certain rules that are to be followed. You are no exception. These assigned labels contribute to who you believe you are. Lots of different factors determine your labels, including the choices you have made, the area you were born in, the people you surround yourself with, your parents, the assumptions set by others and of course your beliefs. These are all reasons for people to judge you and therefore label you.

It all starts when you are very young. When the world tells you that to be a good kid, you must behave a certain way, walk a certain line. The benefits of being a good kid are desirable to most children: rewards from parents, society and teachers. There is nothing wrong with that, the problem is that those children who express themselves outside the line are labeled bad. The idea that a person, child or not, lives with color, walking to their own beat, creates a threat to those inside the box. So, a label must be developed for those who don't comply to these standards. This label, is more often than not, "bad" and/or faulty. A perfect example of where this labeling really starts to define who we are is in the public school system.

My nephew has been labeled one of these "bad" kids because he is hyperactive, learns differently and expresses his individuality. His 2nd grade teacher made it known that if he wanted to stay in her class, he needed to be on medication. This has really become protocol for anyone outside the box. They are labeled and medicated back into that box. In many cases, these kids being labeled as "bad" begin to believe that it is true. They give up on themselves and act out, working to live up to the labels they have been given.

I was personally labeled when I was sixteen years old and became pregnant. I was instantly labeled negatively. Society assumes that you will drop out of high school, live on state aid and struggle the rest of your life. I had my daughter at age seventeen and I was treated very poorly by teachers, other parents, doctors and society in general. The label I was given was that I would not amount to anything and I actually had a counselor in my high school tell me that I needed to get real about my future because I would never have a successful life. I never listened. I am determined to let my actions define me and not the labels placed by outside influences. So here I am today living my dream, finding success in all that I do, teen mother and all!

Life Check 3-1: Old Labels

✓ What labels have you been given by society, your parents, other outside sources?

✓ Do you live up to the labels given to you by others? Do you believe them to be true?

✓ What steps can you take to prove that those labels are false?

Societal labels do not merit truth. If you listen to the labels you have been given, they can be very discouraging and may be keeping you limited with the feeling that you have to live up to them. I've seen many people who stay stuck in their idea of who they are because society, a friend or family member told them that is what they were. For some people, success seems like an impossible feat after growing up in a small town and watching their parents struggle to make ends meet. They feel that's all there is to life. So they never aspire to anything more.

Life Check 3-2: New Labels

✓ List all you aspire to become, all labels aside. The bigger, the better.

✓ What actions can you start today to move closer to creating the label you want?

There is also the factor of allowing people who you are close with to determine who you believe you are. Take a moment to think about the five people you spend most of your time with. These five people are invited into your daily living by you, so they must be great, right? It is the people closest to you who can cause the most damage, if you allow it. They know how to build you up as well as how to tear your down. Every day you spend with someone who brings you down takes away from living a life full of potential. Be aware of the attitudes and words being said by those you spend your time with.

If you have a toxic friend or family member who is always negative and belittling you, it is time to send them on their way. Honor yourself by removing anyone who doesn't appreciate your greatness, because the more you hear their negativity the more you may start to believe it.

Life Check 3-3: V.I.P.s

Take an inventory of the 5 people you spend most of your time with. These five people have the most influence on you as a person. Are these positive, motivating people or negative, draining people? They directly affect your daily living. How do they contribute to your life?

Name   **Contribution**

1._____

2._____

3._____

4._____

5._____

Now, I hope that when you have listed your five people, you did not forget to list yourself. After all, you are with yourself all of the time. Your life will reflect whether you constantly doubt yourself and degrade your dreams or if you have confidence in all that you do.

Choose to surround yourself with people who support your dreams and encourage your strength. Do not feel guilty because you choose to remove toxic people from your life. Whether it is a relative, friend, employer or significant other, if they are taking away from your confidence by belittling you, then it is time for them to go. If they are not willing to respect your feelings and continue to treat you in an unhealthy way, then it is up to you to stand your ground by removing them from your life. People can only treat you how you let them. Demand respect. Allow nothing less, you are worth it.

Others can project their ideas of a label to you, but in order for a label to stick you must accept it as yours. Yes, your voice is the most powerful because you decide whether to accept a label as your truth or not.

Life Check 3-4: Living the Label

✓ Figure out some appointed labels you have been living with?

✓ Whose voice determined them?

Once you have accepted a label as your truth, you begin to define yourself by it. It becomes part of your internal dialogue, the voice you have with yourself. You work to live up to the label and your inner voice wants to help you out by reassuring you that you are whatever you think you are. It never quits, however much you can try and quiet it. In fact I challenge you to stop right now and try to quiet your inner voice. Can you do it? I know I haven't been able to. It is what you are thinking right now in this moment and in every moment. What is your voice saying right now? You might be thinking about your labels, or this book, or what's for dinner. All of this chatter is your inner dialogue.

The talks you have with yourself are the most powerful influence in your life. What you speak to yourself is your truth, so be conscious of what you are saying about yourself. In many cases you use your internal dialogue to criticize yourself, giving value to what others have said you are. If you are constantly telling yourself that you are not enough, you will eventually believe it. When you find you are attacking yourself with negative words it is important to stop yourself. A great way to do that is to literally say out loud "STOP", after you have said this find a kind, positive word to replace the negativity with—this creates an action and will make you aware of how you are treating yourself. Giving you the opportunity to reprogram your inner voice. Do not ever talk down to yourself. There are enough people out there who will try to discourage you, you surely do not need to do it to yourself.

Life Check 3-5: Negative vs. Positive

✓ Write down all the things you refuse to accept in your life. Include all areas of your life; career, relationships, family.

✓ Evaluate the conversations you are having with yourself. Are they positive or negative?

✓ Replace any negative words you are speaking to yourself with a positive word.

It is time to reprogram that inner voice to empower and motivate you. Raise your standards for yourself and for those you allow in your life, so you will approach it with a new attitude.

Your choice of attitude determines everything in your life including your accomplishments and disappointments. It is your superpower, an amazing action that can and will shift everything for you. The perception with which you see the world and yourself is how you will interpret life. If you are approaching your situations with a negative attitude, then you can expect what you believe. When life hands you lemons, instead of making lemonade you will moan and complain about how unfair it is that you only have lemons. It's always easy to find something to complain about, something that isn't right for you. Life may feel unfair and you didn't get a fair shake because your family was poor, or you're a teen mother, or whatever label you have been carrying around with you.

Approaching life with a new attitude opens doors where walls used to be, allowing you a new outlook and the power to live fully. Making the choice to stop living with limits and shifting your perception to positivity will change the direction of your life to success. You will witness things starting to be a little bit brighter, a little bit better and then super fantastic!

Life Check 3-6: Make Your Own Label

✓ Explore the good in your life, and you will attract more of it.

✓ Evaluate the labels you have collected by outside influences and decide how they are limiting you.

✓ Shift those limiting labels and start creating your own. Whatever you choose to be, that's your label.

It is time to raise the bar by changing what you demand of yourself, what you want out of life and what you will tolerate from those around you. No longer allow yourself to be defined by labels that were given to you by outside influences: you are your own brand. You are a big deal and this life is designed for you. How you live it is in your hands. Do not strive to be average, because you are worth so much more.

4 – Push The Limits

> "We are all living in cages,
> with the door wide open."
>
> ~George Lucas

Finding personal success means pushing the limits. To live with an open mind challenges your personal truth. As you grow, you are taught certain rights and wrongs that become the structure for what you believe, your foundation for life. These lessons are taught to you by the people you spend time with. As a child, you learn most of these rights and wrongs from your parents and other family members. A lot of what you learn as a child is passed down from generation to generation. As you get older, you begin to gain influences from your peers and teachers. It is time to reevaluate what you have been taught throughout the years, and decide what works for you and what doesn't.

Your life is full of learning moments that can change your beliefs, and if you are quick to shut off your mind to anything new you will stay stagnant, with no room for progress. The world is a really big place and there are so many different ideas, concepts and beliefs to explore. Take time to embrace the moments you are presented with to grow, expand and learn something new.

Life Check 4-1: Core Beliefs

✓ Take a moment to look at what your core beliefs are and where they have come from. Examine the beliefs that you hold about love, religion, who you are, your morals and values.

✓ Are your core beliefs something you agree with, or have they been programmed for years into your foundation by society, parents, school, etc.?

Pushing the limits raises the question of who you are vs. who the world tells you to be. So who do you choose to be? As you look at your beliefs and start to evaluate what is real to you and what you have been programmed with, you might be really surprised at how many things you have been practicing that are no longer your truth. Let go of programmed beliefs that no longer serve you. Times have changed and the world is a lot different today compared to forty years ago or even ten years ago. And a lot of the old rigid ideas that may have been the truth in the past have been reinvented, allowing opportunity for growth as a society and as an individual. It is only natural to reevaluate your beliefs now. You may find you are not living your truth, because you are too busy living the truth of your parents or other people. For example think about your career.

Life Check 4-2: Career for Life

✓ What career have you chosen for your life right now?

✓ How did you decide this was the right career path for you? Does it lead back to your parents, your clergy, your third grade teacher?

✓ Or did you pick this career because whenever you thought about it, a spark ignited in your soul?

It can be easy to get caught up in trying to please your parents and the people who you hold in high regard. After all, they have provided for you, drove you where you needed to go and helped you throughout your life. So, choosing a career that makes them smile is the least you can do, right? No, if you are not doing something that makes you happy you are losing part of yourself and not living fully. You will never be happy by making your life choices based on what will please others. You will lose that passion we talked about in chapter one, and life will be boring.

Life Check 4-3: Motivation

✓ Are you less than motivated in any area of your life?

✓ Are you starting to lose your passion for living?

If you answered yes, then it is time to really look at the choices you are making. Are they for you, or to please others?

When you are not living from a place of personal truth you don't receive the full potential you deserve. You are merely pretending to be someone you are not. This is how important exploring your truth is. Weed through all the beliefs that no longer serve you, and get rid of them to live from an authentic place, experiencing a passion for life! You will know when this happens because you'll be inspired and motivated on incredible levels. You will be so filled with passion that you can move mountains.

While you are going through this process, be prepared to face others who don't understand why you are getting rid of old beliefs. These people are still very much living with them, and have no desire to change anything. The natural response from those people will be to attack and belittle you back to the old ways. Keep strong and do not waver. Whenever you push the limits to change yourself, it intimidates and threatens those who are not ready. This is not your problem although the people attacking you will want you to feel that it is. It won't do you any good to try to convince them to see your point of view if they are not ready.

I went through this as I started to change myself. I watched as family and friends dropped like flies. Sometimes I questioned myself and thought maybe something was wrong with me. Then I looked at the whole picture and saw that the people that were leaving me weren't ready for positive change. As soon as I started displaying respect for myself and demanding it from others, they were out. Now, who wants to be surrounded by people who do not respect them? I know I don't, and every person who has left my life has opened a door for someone else who does respect me. I am grateful.

When dealing with these people, it will do you good to create healthy boundaries. You don't have to cut them out of your life completely, but just monitor how much time you spend together. If every time you get together it turns into a battle of "I am right, you are wrong" then maybe you need to reevaluate the relationship. Removing negative people from your daily living doesn't mean you don't love them, but that you honor and respect yourself too much to allow their negativity to intrude on your life. Allow them their space to be who they are, but don't allow them to take one ounce of who you are. Continue to live your personal truth, allowing opportunity for growth and expansion in all areas of your life.

Life Check 4-4: Challenge Your Beliefs

✓ Explore your beliefs. Do not be afraid to challenge them, removing some and replacing others.

✓ Set healthy boundaries with those who do not support you.

5 – Setting Life In Motion

"One day you will wake up and there won't be any more time to do the things you've always wanted. Do it now."

~Paulo Coelho

Are you ready to live the life you've imagined; the life you dreamed about, talked about? This is the life in which you accomplish all you set out to, taking the world by storm. Living with intense happiness, working your dream job, living in the most amazing house, experiencing life to its full potential... this is the life that you envisioned when you were growing up.

Life Check 5-1: Re-imagine Life

✓ Are you living the life you imagined, or did you give up on that idea?

✓ Are you ready to get that life back?

It is time to quit talking about having all that you desire and to really start experiencing all that life has to offer you.

The most powerful way to get things moving in a positive direction is to create some goals, focusing your intentions toward what you want. Big or small, the important thing is to reach for something, and to create the situation you desire. You cannot reach a destination without a location in mind, and the same is true for becoming successful. Goals are your road map to that success.

Life Check 5-2: Direction

What direction do you need to go in order to accomplish what you want?

    ✓ Without goals, you are only searching for a way instead of working toward making something happen. All of your aspirations are available to you as long as you are willing to get up and do the work to achieve them.

Life Check 5-3: Goals

✓ What are your goals? Make a list for each area of your life, including personal, career and family areas.

You have to take action if you expect to accomplish anything. Be willing to get your hands dirty . Creating an action plan will get you from point A to the finish line. Break your goal into steps so you don't become overwhelmed by what needs to be done to get there. Each step leads you closer to accomplishing what you want.

From deciding what you want to taking action, each step is a must do. Just insert your goal and get to making it happen!

Life Check 5-4: "Making it Happen" Plan

✓ **Step 1~** Decide what you want. This sounds easy, but sometimes when you are traveling down the road of life, you aren't completely clear on your desires. A great indicator that you are headed in a positive direction is when are working towards something that you feel deep within your spirit, that gets you excited when you think about it. It could be as small as taking a daily walk to as big as being the president of the United States. The goal size doesn't matter, what matters is the inspiration and determination you gain from it.

✓ **Step 2~** Break your goal into steps. Achieving your goals can seem overwhelming. Taking the time to plan it out in steps will make it manageable. You will be able to see your goal from an obtainable viewpoint and as you complete each step you will feel a sense of accomplishment.

✓ **Step 3~** Take action. The only way anything happens is by you taking action. You can list your goals and break them into achievable steps, but if you continue to just sit on the couch, then you are guaranteed to achieve nothing. To be most effective, correlate your actions to the steps you have listed above.

After you have created yourself an effective 3 step plan to set your goals in motion, you must figure out how determined you are to making them happen. It's easy to write out what you need to do, it is a different story finding the motivation within yourself to follow through without becoming distracted.

You know those days when you wake up and are ready to go, and your feet hit the ground running. You are determined and motivated to make stuff happen, but as the day goes on you start to get distracted by other things and start to waver from your goal. You find other things you need to do and slowly forget the direction you were heading, so your goal is put on the back burner for that day. You reassure yourself, you'll get back to it. Unfortunately that doesn't always happen because life takes over, and your goals become an afterthought. You must commit to your goals by staying determined and motivated.

Life Check 5-5: Goal Management

✓ Start to visualize how you will accomplish your goal. Envision yourself taking these steps and accomplishing what you need from each one. Practicing this vision for twenty minutes a day will empower you, inspiring your spirit and motivating you back toward your goals.

✓ Post notes everywhere that outline your goals and the results you will achieve by accomplishing them. Have them around your house, in your car, on your desk at work.

✓ Manage your time. Set aside a certain allotment of time each day to work on your goals. The most common way to get distracted from achieving your goals is to allow your time to be frittered away. Too often they become afterthoughts. Taking time each day to work toward accomplishing what you desire will bring you closer to making it happen.

✓ Commit to doing 5 things a day to make your goals happen. Start a journal to document these.

Your determination will decide if your goals come to life or not. To spark that fire again, look back at your goals and think about why you wanted them and what you are willing to do to get them. Then go do it!

6 – Lose Sight of the Shore

"You can never cross the ocean unless you have
the courage to lose sight of the shore."

~Christopher Columbus

In order to see what is available out there, you must have the self-confidence to lose sight of the shore. The harbor is safe of course, and you are familiar with it, but in order to really experience life and all it has to offer, you must take risks. You must find the confidence to make this happen.

This will allow you to let go of self-doubt and start to believe that you are enough and you deserve all the world has to offer, giving you the confidence to step outside of your comfort zone and into your greatness! Have you ever been in a room when a confident person walks in? You can feel it. It shines like the sun. It draws others to them because everyone wants to feel that way within themselves.

You cannot become confident by rubbing up against a confident person, but must find that inner beauty within yourself. You have it, it is time to awaken it!

Life Check 6-1: Self-Belief

✓ Do you believe in yourself?

✓ Are you that confident, shining person? Or are you the person sunbathing in the confident glow of others?

Believing in yourself is a vital part of your existence. It really doesn't matter if ten thousand others believe in you, if you do not see, feel and know your greatness, you will not live a confident lifestyle. Confidence encourages you to accept yourself as whole with love and respect. A powerful human being full of inspiration, determination and motivation, an unstoppable force!

By realizing and accepting your confidence, you are able to shine in the areas that are important to you. You can let go of the fear of not fitting in, and really embrace your true self, giving you freedom. What others think of you becomes minor compared to the empowerment you feel within. Strengthening your inner being will replace any and all doubt you may have been experiencing, allowing you to live with self-love and power.

Confident people don't judge or label others as being inferior. They look within and discover they hold their power and greatness. Confident people understand there is no need to take away anything from anyone else to feel better about themselves.

When you are confident you expect great things from life. You realize that life is full of amazing opportunities, you see the beauty that surrounds you, and you want some of that in your daily living.

You start to invite great things into your life. Attracting more of what makes you feel good leaves no room for anything that takes away from living well. Opportunities are everywhere! If one door closes, you do not sit down and give up, you climb through the window because you know life conspires to give you what you want. Be always ready and willing for whatever comes your way.

Life Check 6-2: Opportunity Knocks

✓ What positive opportunities are surround-
ing you?

✓ What great things are you inviting into
your life?

Many times, you can feel discouraged to get
out there and take a risk because you may fail. The
most important information to have if you are
feeling this way is that failures do not exist.
Failing is not a reality. Each time you make the
effort to do or accomplish something and you
learn from that experience, it is a success. You are
learning a lesson, gaining knowledge, which is
what life is all about.

Even though the outcome may not be what you
expected and you did not get exactly what you
wanted, it doesn't mean you have not learned
something valuable. You learned what didn't
work, so the next time your find yourself in that
situation, you will try something new. You must
get back up and try again. Use your experiences as
trial and error. Anyone who has ever become
successful in life used their not so successful
experiences to propel themselves to the next level
of competence.

For example, you have heard of the amazing
Walt Disney and his legacy. Although success was
not always his, he used each loss as a stepping
stone to his ultimate success. His rough start not
only included being fired from a newspaper

because the editor thought he lacked imagination, he also got involved with some other businesses that had little to no success and ended up bankrupt. These experiences could have been enough for him to quit and give up, but thankfully he used what he had learned and continued to try until he created success for himself.

A great many stories like this illustrate the point that there is no good time to quit. Learn from your experiences and use them as stepping stones to get you to where you want to go. The only time failure has an effect on your life is when you choose to stay down, stuck in what you have not accomplished.

> If you can dream it, you can do it.
> Remember that this whole thing was
> started with a dream and a mouse"
> ~ Walt Disney

Life Check 6-3: Starting Over!

✓ What aspiration have you given up on because you were knocked down?

✓ How can you revisit that goal, using your experiences as stepping stones to start moving toward accomplishing it?

Now that you are back up and running toward personal success, you must to be willing to jump off the cliff and take the risks. There are so many opportunities lost because of fear. This can be the fear of not making it, the fear of what others will say, the fear of fear. You can become disabled by the thoughts you create in your mind. Letting go of the limiting thoughts and making the choice to risk it all will lead you directly to success. Be "all in" for your life. Those times when you feel scared of what might happen, remind yourself that you haven't come this far to quit now. The world awaits all that you have to offer.

7 – Live Today to Create Tomorrow

"Don't let yesterday use up too much today."
~Will Rogers

Life Check 7-1: 24 hours

Today is your day, you have been given twenty-four hours to do anything you want.

✓ How will you spend your time?

✓ What will you trade your twenty-four hours for?

Time is the most valuable commodity in existence, and it will not stop for anyone. It is the same for us all. It doesn't matter how much money you have, what your career is or how powerful you are—time will not stop. If you are repeating stories of the past, you will lose all your time in the present.

I know you have some great memories from your past that make you feel important when you talk about them. It is great to relive those moments occasionally, but it is important to experience your life the now.

For example, you know that guy who was the quarterback of his high school football team and is always telling the story of how he made that winning touchdown in 1989 and he recalls it play by play and constantly repeats it to everyone he knows, bragging about how he was so awesome and it was the best time of his life. He repeats this story every time there is a get-together or anytime he runs into anyone he knows in the grocery store. Or there may be your girlfriend who can't quit talking about how she used to be such fun back in the old days, dancing on the bars, getting her drinks for free, staying up until four in the morning and doing it all over again the next night. To her that was when she was really "living the life".

People who are stuck repeating their "glory day" stories are doing so because the life they have created in the now is not good. Instead of looking at where they are now, they choose to pretend they are still living in that moment, hoping that others still see them as that winning quarterback or fun party girl.

Life Check 7-2: Yesterday

- ✓ Are you wasting today by holding on to who you were yesterday?

- ✓ Do you repeat the stories from your "glory days" to everyone you know, every chance you get?

So much of your now can be lost if you are busy reminiscing about who you used to be, and how much fun you used to have. If you don't have any great stories to share in the present, it is because of the life you have chosen to live, the choices you have made to this point in your life. It's not too late to start living your now with passion.

Life Check 7-3: Stories

- ✓ What stories are you creating in the present?

- ✓ Are you satisfied today or would you like to go back to when you were twenty?

Personally I would not want to go back to when I was twenty. The person I was then does not compare to who I am today. The stories I have to tell now outdo anything I did then. I appreciate the life lessons and growth that has brought me to my present self. I want to spend my *now* time focusing on- What I can create in the present.

It is time to focus on your now. Let go of that old you and replace it with the new and improved you who is living fully in the moment. Take the time to slow down and seize the moment by recognizing all that you have to offer in the present. Acknowledge your greatness and accept that life is *now*.

~

Life Check 7-4: There is Only Now!

✓ What can you do in this moment to take immediate control of your present?

✓ What new amazing life stories will you create, starting today?

This moment right here, this moment is your life. Live it fully!

Epilogue

You have been given this one life and what you do with it is up to you. Stand up today for what you believe! Shining bright for all the world to see.

It is easy to lose sight of what you are worth by listening to the opinions of others, of what society believes, of what we think we should be. Most of the stress and unhappiness in your life is because you have created an idea of what you think you are supposed to be, instead of allowing life to be lived. Face it, things change, people change and yet you are afraid of accepting the person you are. It is time to start seeing your worth for what it is. You are an amazing, beautiful, complete person— no matter your childhood or your past choices.

Today, take a moment to really appreciate your worth. Look at yourself in the mirror and state, "I Am Worth IT." If at first you do not believe it, that is OK. Self doubt happens, but it is imperative that you replace the judging with acceptance. You will see that the more you practice this, the more it will become your truth. You can forever change the way you look at yourself and how you live your life. Do this daily, hourly, every opportunity you get. You are worth it and I believe in you!

Love, Gratitude & Kindness
Robin Marvel

About the Author

Robin Marvel is "that" girl. She has survived mental, domestic and drug abuse, homelessness and kidnappings throughout her childhood. Becoming addicted to alcohol and partying at age 15 resulted in a sexual assault and to becoming a teen mother at age 16 (not because of the sexual assault).

Upon finding out she was having a girl, she made the choice that they would not be a statistic. She knew she would have to work hard and continue to work hard to make sure that would become her truth. By living with self-respect and determination, Robin strives to be a positive role model for her 5 daughters.

She has taken those negative situations she was dealt in life, and turned them into motivation and purpose.

Now a multi-published author and motivational speaker in the field of self development, her passion is to use her story to show others that they are not a product of their past, to show them that even though they may face challenges, they have the power to live their dreams by breaking cycles and taking personal responsibility now. She is proof of this!

She has also started a non-profit organization, S.E.L.F—Self Empowered Living Free. This

involves striving to create strength and confidence
through aiding those in need. S.E.L.F. hosts a
variety of charitable events to fill food pantries,
provide life skills and empowerment to those in
need. It focuses on the homeless, feeding the
hungry and on teen pregnancy.

She invites you to visit her website at
www.robinmarvel.com to learn more.

Bibliography

Dyer, W. (2001). *10 Secrets for Success and Inner Peace*. Carlsbad, CA :Hay House

Dyer, W. (2006). *Inspiration: your ultimate calling*. Carlsbad, CA : Hay House

Lambert, M. (2005). *Natural highs for body & soul: Instant energizers to banish everyday energy lows*. London: Hamlyn. (Motivation, Self-Help)

MacLean, K. J. (2006). *The vibrational universe: Harnessing the power of thought to consciously create your life*. Ann Arbor, Mi: Loving Healing Press. (motivational, self help)

Marvel, R. (2008). *Awakening consciousness: A girl's guide!"* 1. Ann Arbor, Mi: Loving Healing Press.

Noyes, R. (2007). *The seven doors*. Gardners Books. (Metaphysical, non-fiction)

Paul, A. (2000). *Girlosophy: A soul survival kit.* Crow's Nest, NSW: Allen & Unwin. (Children's Books, Self Help)

Petrinovich, T. S. (2002). *The call: Awakening the angelic human.* [United States]: Sar'h Pub. House. (metaphysical, motivation)

Ray, V. (1991). *Choosing happiness: The art of living unconditionally*. New York, NY:

HarperCollins Publishers.

Ruiz, Don Miguel (2011). *The fifth agreement: A practical self guide to self mastery*. Amber-Allen Publishing (Toltec Wisdom)

Seuss. (1990). *Oh, the places you'll go!* New York: Random House. (Children's Book)

Shane, S. (2006). *Spiritually awake in the physical world*. [United States]: Liquid Light Center. (metaphysical, motivation)

Silverstein, S. (1964). *The giving tree*. New York: Harper & Row.

Stein, D. (1987). *The woman's book of healing*. The Crossing Point: Berkeley, CA (self help)

Tolle, E. (2005). *A new earth: Awakening to your life's purpose*. New York, N.Y.: Dutton/Penguin Group. (self-help)

Vaishāli. (2006). *You are what you love*. [S.l.]: Purple Haze Press.

Wing, D. L. (2010). *The true nature of tarot*. Ann Arbor, MI.: Marvelous Spirit Press (Metaphysical, Self Help)

Wolfe, A. (2003) *In the shadow of the shaman: Connecting with self, nature & spirit*. St. Paul, MN : Llewellyn (Self Help)

Index

truth, 43
victims, 11–14
VIPs, 34–35
who you are, 2

wounded eye, 9–10, 12
yesterday, 68

Notes

Empowering Books from Robin Marvel

Reshaping Reality will encourage you to shake your spirit awake from anything that is limiting you from your potential, propelling you into a life of purpose and meaning, giving you the support needed to grow, evolve, and empower your life.

Today, you stop existing and start L-I-V-I-N-G.

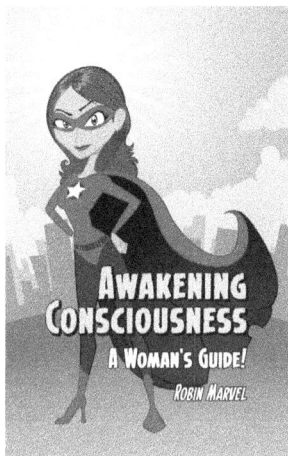

This guide will strengthen and encourage you to discover your inner core and create an empowered zest for life.

The exercises and crafts in this hands-on guide have been designed to Awaken your Consciousness on your path of self-awareness. ultimate love, tranquility and strength for your mind, body and soul.

www.ingramcontent.com/pod-product-compliance
Lightning Source LLC
Chambersburg PA
CBHW030027290326
41934CB00005B/514